Cinco de Mayo

Aurora Colón García

Heinemann Library
Chicago, Illinois

Customer Service 888–454–2279
Visit our website at www.heinemannlibrary.com

Page layout by Jennifer Lee
Printed and bound in the United States by Lake Book Manufacturing, Inc.

07 06 05 04
10 9 8 7 6 5 4 3 2

Library of Congress Cataloging-in-Publication Data
Colón García, Aurora.
  Cinco de Mayo / Aurora Colón García.
     p. cm. -- (Holiday histories)
Summary: Discusses the holiday Cinco de Mayo, celebrated by Mexicans and Mexican Americans in remembrance of the Mexican army's defeat of the French army in Pubela, Mexico, in 1862.
Includes bibliographical references and index.
  ISBN 1-4034-3501-4 (HC), 1-4034-3686-X (Pbk.)
  1. Cinco de Mayo (Mexican holiday)--History--Juvenile literature. 2. Mexico--Social life and customs--Juvenile literature. 3. Mexican Americans--Social life and customs--Juvenile literature. 4. Cinco de Mayo, Battle of, 1862--Juvenile literature. [1. Cinco de Mayo (Mexican holiday) 2. Mexico--Social life and customs. 3. Holidays.] I. Title. II. Series.
  F1233.C6523 2003
  394.262--dc21
                           2003007825

Acknowledgments
The author and publishers are grateful to the following for permission to reproduce copyright material:

Cover photograph by David Young-Wolff/PhotoEdit

p. 4 Eric Miller/AP Wide World Photo; p. 5 Damian Dovarganes/AP Wide World Photo; p. 6 Bill Bachmann/Index Stock Imagery; p. 7 Charlene E. Friesen/DDB Stock; pp. 9, 29 Stewart Attchison/DDB Stock; pp. 10, 11 Joe Luis Magana/AP Wide World Photo; pp. 12, 13, 24 The Granger Collection, NY; pp. 14, 15, 17, 18, 26 Hulton Archive/Getty Images; p. 16 Corbis; pp. 19, 25 Bettmann/Corbis; pp. 20, 22 Richard Cummins/Corbis; p. 21 Charles & Josette Lenars/Corbis; p. 23 Virginia Ferrero/DDB Stock; p. 27 Carl & Ann Purcell/Corbis; p. 28 Aultman Collection/El Paso Public Library/AP Wide World Photo; p. 29 Stewart Aitchison/DDB Stock Photo

Photo research by Kathy Creech

Some words are shown in bold, **like this.** You can find out what they mean by looking in the glossary.

Contents

A Day for Celebrating

¡Viva Cinco de Mayo! On May 5 floats are decorated. Dancers, singers, and children dressed in festive clothing ride on the floats in the parades.

4

Many Mexican-Americans celebrate their
heritage on this day. They celebrate with
parades, **festivals,** music, and dancing.
They celebrate **pride** and **freedom.**

Celebrations from City to City

Cinco de Mayo is celebrated all across the country. The holiday is celebrated in Chicago, Denver, San Antonio, and many other cities.

In San Antonio, Texas, many people may clap to the beat of the popular Latino groups performing their music or dances on stage in Market Square.

Celebrations in Mexico

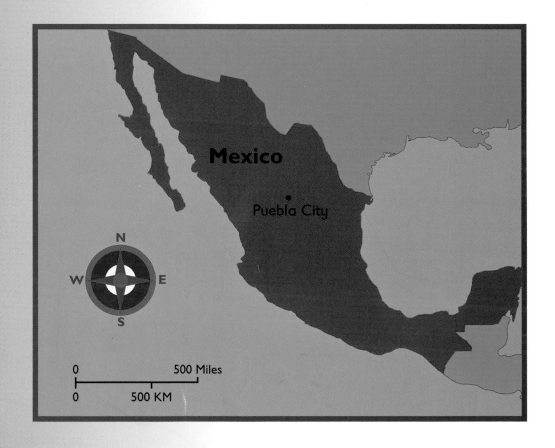

In the country of Mexico, many Mexicans celebrate Cinco de Mayo in a city called Puebla. Cinco de Mayo is also celebrated in many other cities in Mexico.

In Mexico, there are **festivals** and parades.
At the festivals food is sold from booths
decorated in bright colors. But why do we
celebrate Cinco de Mayo?

Why Do We Celebrate?

Cinco de Mayo means May 5 in Spanish. A long time ago on May 5, 1862 a **battle** took place in Puebla, Mexico. This holiday celebrates the Mexican army winning the battle against the French army.

Cinco de Mayo celebrates the **unity** and **pride** of the Mexican people. Today at the **festivals** men dress up as soldiers and pretend to have a fight. Mexico always wins in these make believe battles.

Mexican Independence

During the 1800's Mexico was under the control of Spain. On September 15, 1810 **Father Miguel Hidalgo** united the Mexican people. He encouraged the Mexicans to fight for their **freedom.**

Mexico was free from Spain in 1821.
They did not know how to run the country.
They had two different groups trying to run
the country. This caused many problems.
The Mexican government was not united.

Mexican-American War

After Mexico was free from Spain, they began to argue with the United States. The United States wanted Mexico's land. Mexico would not give up its land. Mexico and the United States went to war.

This war was the Mexican-American War.
The United States won the war. Mexico
had to give up half of its land to the
United States.

Money Trouble

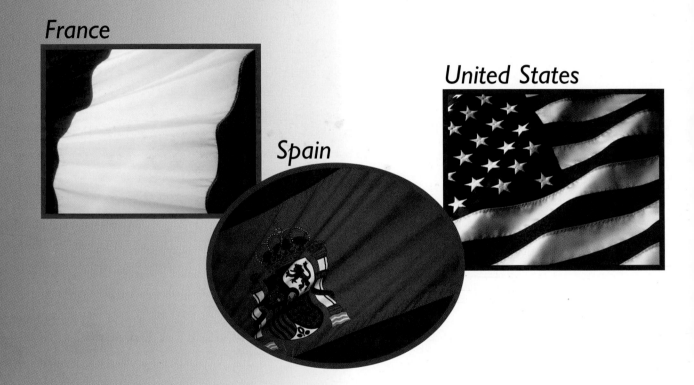

France

Spain

United States

After the Mexican-American War, Mexico had very little money in its **treasury.** They used a lot of their money on the many **battles** they fought. Mexico owed money to France, Spain, and the United States.

Benito Juárez was the president. He told the
other countries he would pay them later.
He used the little money Mexico had to
help the people.

France

Napoleon III was the ruler of France.
He was very angry when Mexico did not
pay. He decided to take land from Mexico.

France wanted to rule Mexico. They
wanted to add Mexico's land to their
government. Napoleon III sent his army
to Mexico to try to take over.

The French Army

France had the strongest and best-trained army. They knew how to fight in **battle** and had good weapons.

In 1861, the French army attacked Vera Cruz, Mexico and won the battle. The French took over Vera Cruz. They began to move towards Puebla.

The Mexican Army

The men in the Mexican army were not well trained. Their weapons were old. The Mexican army was small. They did not know how to fight in **battles.**

This statue of General Ignacion Zaragoza stands in Puebla, Mexico.

President Benito Juárez sent General Ignacion Zaragoza and his soldiers to Puebla to stop the French soldiers. He led the brave men in the Mexican army into battle.

23

The Battle of Puebla

General Zaragoza put his men on the two
hills outside the city of Puebla. The French
soldiers went up the hills to attack the
Mexican solidiers. The brave Mexican soldiers
fired their **muskets** and cannons at them.

The French soldiers went back down the hill. During the **battle** it begun to rain. The rain made it hard for the French soldiers to comeback up the hills. The sides of the hills turned into mud. The French **retreated.**

★

Victory for the Mexicans

The Mexican soldiers fought hard. They won the **battle** against the powerful French army. The battle was called the La Batalla de Puebla. The Mexican people finally had a **common cause.**

Mexicans were proud to say, "Yo soy Mexicano!" It was a victory against great odds!

An American Celebration

Later, many Mexicans began to move to United States to find jobs. When they came to the states they bought along their **customs** and celebrations.

Their celebrations has become part
of the American culture.

Important Dates

Cinco de Mayo

1810	Father Miguel Hidalgo unite the Mexicans
1821	Mexican gain independence from Spain
1846	Mexican-American War
1861	Vera Cruz surrenders to the French
1862	Battle of Puebla
1960s	Mexican-American students at California State University, Los Angeles, holds the first Cinco de Mayo celebration.
1995	Greater East Austin Youth League begins the annual Austin Cinco de Mayo music festival.

Glossary

battle a fight between armies

common cause a supported movement

custom a usual way of doing something

festival a celebration

heritage birthright

muskets a large heavy gun

pride having self-respect

retreated to withdraw

treasury where the governemnt keeps its money

untrained not prepared or instructed

unity to stand together

More Books to Read

Flanagan, Alice K. *Cinco de Mayo*. Minneapolis, MN: Compass Point, 2003.

MacMillan, Dinne M. Mexican Independence Day and Cinco de Mayo. Berkeley Heights, New Jersey:Enslow Publishers, Inc., 1997.

Winchester, Faith. Hispanic Holidays.Mankato, Minnesota:Capstone Press, 1996.

Index